Everyday Mediterranean

Everyday Mediterranean

Food, life and living longer the Mediterranean way

with healthy oil

Mary Valle

Contents

For my family in Greece who give
with open hands, thank you...

Acknowledgement

A very big and humble thank you to everyone, family and friends, who helped me, supported and encouraged me in putting this book together.

To my publisher, Diane, thank you for the possibility and all your support along the way. To the entire creative team at New Holland, Fiona, Olga, Holly and Andy thankyou for your vision and creativity. A humble thank you from the bottom of my heart.

Thank you to Greg for his gorgeous photography and to Georgia for her creative imagination. It was lots of fun.

To my friends Maryanne and Susan and my nephew David who rolled up their sleeves and helped in the kitchen... a very big and heartfelt thanks for all your love, support and much needed help.

To my precious family, Sarah, Rebecca and Paul, Catherine and Robert, Steven and Melissa... you are everything.

Mary x

A note from the author...

I remember the first time I went to Greece, I was a little nervous but excited at the same time. It was summer and the vegetable gardens were abundant with tomatoes, cucumbers, zucchini, greens and herbs; flowers in bloom, framing footpaths and roads – it was a delicious garden. From that very first moment, the importance of fresh, seasonal produce and a way of life became clearer to me.

Every time I go to Greece, it never fails to surprise me with the intensity of flavors in every piece of fruit or vegetable that you eat. Tomatoes so sweet, all they need is to be cut in half, drizzled with olive oil and sprinkled with a pinch of salt; salads accompanying every meal with the simplest of dressings, a drizzle of olive oil, a squeeze of a lemon and a pinch of salt; bowls of sweet cherries for dessert, or refreshing slices of watermelon.

I love the traditional recipes that are prepared all over Greece, using similar ingredients and often exactly the same but somehow a little different, depending on the hands that prepared it, of course, everyone owning their recipe as the original version.

I remember a woman saying once, 'what grows together, goes together'. Vegetables and herbs growing at the same time in the same place, picked and prepared together – the best in seasonal harmony.

The ritual every morning after breakfast was a walk to the markets to buy ingredients for the day's meal, lunch being the main meal of the day – stopping for a coffee along the way was a must.

For me, Mediterranean ingredients speak for themselves, always use the best seasonal produce you can get your hands on and prepare simply... glorious.

Introduction

Our family table always reflected our culture, and my mother's Greek Mediterranean cuisine, these are the flavors of my childhood. As a mother and a cook myself, my kitchen continues with an abundance of these flavors, the mesmerizing aromas, nourishing soups and the ultimate comfort foods that I grew up with.

The Greek Mediterranean plate is not only about the food but also about the lifestyle. The importance of this lifestyle is evident from the research into the longevity of the people who live in the Mediterranean and around the Aegean Sea. Some of these islands have been known as 'islands where people forget to die'. This poses the question why the people of these islands live so long: what is the secret to a long life?

The enjoyment of a Mediterranean diet seems to be the key; it has often been referred to as the healthiest way to eat. It is rich in excellent olive oil, the best yogurt, whole grains, fish and seafood, sun-kissed seasonal fruit and vegetables, wild greens and bean dishes often being the main meal and not as a side, salads being a part of every meal, and fruit always following the main, small portions of meat and cheeses.

Seasonal food and the integrity of the ingredients are the foundation – the perfect way to eat: simple, healthy and delicious.

What I also find interesting is that the Mediterranean diet follows a lifestyle which holds the importance of strong social connections – spending time with family and friends, as well as daily physical activity, which could be as simple as making walking part of your daily routine, and taking a nap in the afternoon, or simply having some quiet time.

I notice this especially whenever spending time with family in Greece. I love the simplicity of life in the village, mealtimes not only being a time to eat, but to spend together, creating a strong bond between family and friends, young and old. I especially love the way that the conversation over breakfast was always about what we would cook for lunch that day. Visiting the local markets for fresh ingredients, or picking vegetables from the veggie patch, soulful meals prepared with love. My Auntie has a saying, and it goes like this: "Eat Greek and live well". I agree with her.

The recipes in this book are a selection of my best loved meals, ones that I have been enjoying most of my life and others that I have discovered along the way.

Take the time to eat well, cherish every moment and, most of all, enjoy!

The ingredients of the Mediterranean diet

Olive oil is the main source of fat

Herbal teas

Eat beans and legumes at least twice a week

Eat fruit everyday for dessert

Eat vegetables with every meal

Eat fruit and vegetables that are in season

Enjoy wild greens

Have a daily nap

Share meals with family and friends at the dinner table

Enjoy fish at least twice a week

Eat poultry at least twice a week

Eat less red meat as a side, or once a week

Drink water

Drink alcohol always with a meal and in moderation

Exercise daily

Strong sense of community

Learn to cook

Eat yogurt everyday and cheese in moderation

Use herbs and spices instead of salt to season foods

Sweets can be for special occasions

Olive Oil

Olive oil is an integral ingredient and the cornerstone of the Mediterranean diet – an 'everyday food'.

Greece is the world's third largest producer of olive oil and a leader in the consumption of it. Most of the olive oil produced in Greece is used domestically and little is exported, Spain being the largest producer of olive oil and Italy the second.

It is rich in monounsaturated fatty acids and is the main source of dietary fat in the Mediterranean diet. Extra virgin and virgin olive oils have a greater health benefit as they retain the majority of the olive fruit's nutrients, it also contains natural antioxidants such as polyphenols and carotenoids and vitamin E. These antioxidants are a protective agent and there have been many studies into the benefits of its consumption. These studies show that people who consume olive oil regularly reduce their risk of cardiovascular disease and stroke as well as having a protective role towards some cancers developing, such as breast and skin cancers. These studies go even further and suggest additional benefits such as maintaining a healthy blood pressure, healthy cholesterol levels, immune function, protection against Alzheimer's disease, diabetes, rheumatoid arthritis, osteoporosis, type 2 diabetes, depression and promoting a healthy weight.

To invite the greatest benefits from olive oil always use fresh, usually 18 months to 2 years from harvest. Once a bottle is opened use within 6 months, this should not be a problem if olive oil becomes an everyday food. It is not just for salads, as some would believe; it is also used in all cooking, stewing, braising, roasting and frying (it has a smoke point high enough for home frying needs). Studies have shown, to receive the benefits of olive oil, you need to consume 2 tablespoons a day, which is not that difficult if you cook with olive oil and use it to dress your salads as well.

There are many varieties of olives, the most important ones being those with a high polyphenol content producing a more stable oil. The Koroneiki variety grown mainly in Crete and in the Peleponese is one of the most important varieties, together with Picual and Conicabra varieties from Spain and Coraina and Moraiolo varieties from Italy.

Olive oil not only provides these health benefits and protective factors: it also enhances the taste of our food. It makes food more palatable and easier to digest. Medical studies show that many nutrients are fat-soluble, not water-soluble, requiring dietary fat to absorb. Therefore, cooking in olive oil not only heightens the nutrients, but also allows for easier absorption.

Wild greens

Wild greens are an organic part of the Mediterranean diet. They are packed with nutrients and a great source of vitamins, minerals, antioxidants, source of omega 3 fatty acids and calcium. Wild greens and olive oil are a perfect marriage. Whether they are cooked in olive oil or dressed with it, the oil assists in the development of their fine flavors. Recent studies show that not only is the flavor enhanced but the health benefits of vegetables are also heightened by adding olive oil onto them, as the oil aids in the absorption of the nutrients, therefore providing the greatest benefits.

Amaranth (Amaranth viridis), known as 'vlita' in Greek, is popular in Greece. There are many varieties of amaranth, sometimes cultivated for its seeds. The leaves are boiled for salads, fillings for pies or used in braises with zucchini, green beans, purslane or potoates.

Dandelion, known as 'radiki' in Greek, is eaten raw as well as cooked in salads and braises.

Nettles, known as 'tsouknida' in Greek, and are always eaten cooked, mainly as fillings in pies.

Arugula (Rocket) known as 'roka' in Greek is used raw in salads or cooked in braises.

Purslane, also known as 'glistrida', is used mainly raw in salads.

Wild fennel, known in Greek as 'marathon', is used in salads, savory pies, fritters and stuffed dishes.

Wild Chicory is known also as 'radiki' in Greek and is boiled for salads.

Beans and Pulses

Beans and pulses are the foundation of the simple, health-giving Greek cuisine.

Since ancient times, this simple ingredient has been feeding Greek families in an economical and wholesome way. Beans and pulses are low in fat, rich in antioxidants and high in fibre, and are an excellent source of protein, which assists in the protection against heart disease, diabetes and some cancers.

Beans and lentils are also an excellent source of iron. The most popular being white beans such as cannellini and butter beans, chickpeas, lentils, black-eyed peas and yellow split peas. They are mashed, baked, added to soups, casseroles and salads and also made into fritters.

As a young girl growing up in a Greek household I remember every Wednesday and Friday beans were on the menu, usually a soup. Whether it was a lentil soup or a white bean soup (*fasolada*), it was a loyal tradition.

Herbal teas

Herbal teas provide not only a comforting drink but also have been known for their healing properties according to myths and traditions.

Greek Mountain Shepherds tea (*sideritis*) has an earthy taste, and using the flowers adds a comforting floral fragrance. This tea is enormously popular in Greece and one that brings back childhood memories, as it was my mother's most loved tea.

Greek families use herbal teas as their remedy for illness, providing aid in times of need from curing colds, respiratory ailments, digestion, assisting the immune system, to calming mild anxiety and as an antioxidant. Sage tea (*faskomilo*) and Camomile are used for calmness. Linden (*tilio*) eases coughs and colds and aids in digestion and calming. Oregano (*rigani*) aids coughs and chest colds.

Herbal teas are easy to prepare. Boil some water, turn off the heat and submerge the dried herbs, cover and allow to rest for a few minutes. Strain and drink with or without honey.

Mezedes — small plates

Sharing small plates of food with family and friends is typical of the Mediterranean cuisine. Whether it is a few olives, some dip and cheese served with fresh bread or more substantial bits of food, it represents a warm hospitality of the people.

Dolmades filled with bulgar wheat

Serves 4 to 6 people

Ingredients

1 lb/500 g vine leaves (preserved in jars, these
   are already blanched)
1 small onion, diced
9 oz/250 g bulgar wheat
3½ oz/100 g sultans or currants
3½ oz/100 g pine nuts
2 heaped tbs fresh mint, finely chopped
2 heaped tbs fresh parsley, finely chopped

Salt, to taste
Freshly ground black pepper, to taste
Lemon
2 fl oz/60 ml olive oil
8½ fl oz/250 ml hot water
Avgolemono – egg and lemon sauce
  (optional, see recipe page 182)

Method

Place the bulgar wheat into a bowl and pour in enough boiling water to cover the bulgar. Cover the bowl and leave for about 20 minutes.

Rinse the vine leaves and trim the stems.

In a frying pan heat the olive oil and sauté the onion, add the prepared bulgar wheat, sultanas, pine nuts, herbs, mix well and season to taste. Take off the heat.

Line a casserole dish with a few vine leaves (use any that have torn or are too small to roll up).

Spoon out 1–2 tablespoons of the bulgar filling and place at the base of a vine leaf, fold in the sides, roll up and place into the casserole dish. Continue to fill the vine leaves and place them in the dish close together so they keep their shape. When finished drizzle a little extra olive oil over and add 8 fl oz/240 ml of water. Place a plate upside down onto the dolmades to keep them in place. Cover and simmer for about 20–30 minutes.

If finishing with the egg and lemon sauce prepare it and add it to the dolmades when cooked, removing the dish from the heat and using the liquid the dolmades were cooked in. Shake the dish to distribute the sauce evenly.

You can simply squeeze a lemon over the dolmades if you prefer instead of the egg and lemon sauce. Serve hot.

Zucchini fritters

Serves 4 to 6 people

Ingredients

Olive oil

32 oz/1 kg zucchini, grated

1 brown onion, grated

3 eggs

2 tbs parsley, finely chopped

2 tbs mint, finely chopped

1 tbs dill, finely chopped

2½ oz/60 g breadcrumbs

3½ oz/100 g feta
   (kefalotiri is also lovely if you prefer)

Salt, to taste

Freshly ground black pepper

Plain flour for coating

Lemon for serving

Method

Salt the grated zucchini and place in a sieve to drain for about an hour.

Remove from the sieve and squeeze out any excess liquid and place into a bowl. Add the grated onion, eggs, herbs, breadcrumbs, feta and season to taste. Combine well. Rest the mixture in the refrigerator for about an hour.

Heat some olive oil in a large frying pan.

Place some plain flour onto a plate or work surface.

Take enough mixture into your hands, shape into fritters and coat with the flour, shaking off any excess. Fry in the heated olive oil for 4–5 minutes or until golden, turning once. Place on absorbent towels and continue cooking fritters in small batches. Do not overcrowd the frying pan.

Serve with a squeeze of lemon.

Tzatziki with dill

Serves 4 to 6 people

Ingredients

17 fl oz/500 ml plain yogurt
2 fl oz/60 ml olive oil
1 cucumber, peeled, seeded and finely chopped
3 cloves of garlic, finely diced
Salt, to taste
4 heaped tbs dill, finely chopped

Method

Line a colander with some muslin and pour the yogurt into it. Allow it to drain for 4–6 hours in the refrigerator.

Place the strained yogurt into a bowl and add the olive oil, cucumber, garlic and dill.

Season to taste and serve with an extra drizzle of olive oil.

Fennel fritters

Ingredients

7 oz/200 g fennel, finely sliced

7 oz/200 g plain flour

3½ oz/100 g breadcrumbs

1 bunch scallions (spring onions), thinly sliced

Salt, to taste

Freshly ground black pepper

1 tbs of parsley, finely chopped

Olive oil for frying

Lemon for serving

Method

Place all the ingredients into a bowl and season well. Mix until all combined.

In a large frying pan heat the olive oil and drop heaped spoonfuls of the fennel mixture into the oil. Cook until golden brown, turning once.

Do not overcrowd the frying pan.

Serve hot.

Stuffed zucchini flowers

Serves 4 to 6 people

Ingredients

16–20 zucchini (courgette) flowers

1 onion, finely chopped

7 oz/200 g rice

2 ripe tomatoes, grated

1 tbs parsley, finely chopped

1 tbs dill, finely chopped

Pinch of dried oregano

2 fl oz/60 ml olive oil

Salt, to taste

Freshly ground pepper

Method

Preheat the oven to 350°F/180°C.

Prepare the zucchini flowers, rinsing and carefully removing the stamen.

In a frying pan heat the olive oil and sauté the onion until soft. Add the rice and mix well coating the rice with the olive oil and about 4 fl oz/120 ml of water. Add the tomatoes, herbs and season to taste. Simmer for 3–4 minutes and allow it to cool for a bit.

Place a tablespoon of the mixture carefully into each zucchini flower and fold tops over. Arrange in a baking dish. When all finished drizzle a little extra olive oil over and pour 4 fl oz/120 ml of water into the baking dish.

Bake for about 20–30 minutes or until cooked. You may need to add more water to the baking dish if it is looking too dry.

Serve warm or at room temperature.

Pickled vegetables

Ingredients

8½ fl oz/250 ml olive oil

¼ cabbage, cut into chunks

3 carrots, peeled and sliced

2 sticks celery, trimmed and sliced

1 medium head of cauliflower, cut into florets

5 oz/150 g sugar

4 pint/2 l white vinegar

4½ oz/125 g sea salt

3 tsp oregano

1 tsp black peppercorns

Method

Wash and cut the vegetables into bite-sized pieces and put aside in a large bowl.

Place 4 pints/2 litres of water, vinegar, sugar, olive oil, oregano, peppercorns and salt into a large saucepan and bring to the boil. Simmer for 4–5 minutes then pour onto the vegetables, cover and allow them to marinate overnight.

Transfer the pickled vegetables into sterilized jars together with the liquid the next day. This will keep in the refrigerator for about two weeks.

Feta and grapes

Ingredients

1 fl oz/30 ml olive oil

½ fl oz/15 ml honey

½ fl oz/15 ml red wine or balsamic vinegar

Salt, to taste

Freshly ground black pepper

17½ oz/500 g grapes (red and green)

3½ oz/100 g feta cheese, cut into chunks

1 tbs fresh mint, roughly chopped

3½ oz/100 g walnuts

Method

In a small bowl or jar combine the olive oil, honey, vinegar and mix well. Season to taste.

Place the grapes and feta cheese into a serving bowl and drizzle with the dressing. Serve with a sprinkling of mint and walnuts.

Eggplant rolls with feta, olives and sundried tomato

Serves 4 to 6 people

Ingredients

2 fl oz/60 ml olive oil

2 large eggplant (aubergines), trimmed and sliced into
  ½ in/1.5 cm thickness lengthways

2½ oz/60 g feta cheese, crumbled

2½ oz/60 g kalamata olives, pitted and diced

12 sundried tomatoes, diced

Small handful of basil leaves

1 tbs parsley, fined chopped

Salt, to taste

Freshly ground black pepper

Method

In a bowl combine the feta, olives, sundried tomatoes, parsley and mint.

Prepare the eggplant and brush the slices with olive oil. Heat a frying pan with a little extra olive oil over a medium heat and fry the eggplant slices, about 2–3 minutes on each side or until cooked. You can also cook the eggplant over a grill or barbeque if you prefer. Allow it to sit on some absorbent paper while cooking the remainder of the eggplant. Season to taste.

Lay out each eggplant slice and place a heaped tablespoon of the feta mixture at the wider end and roll up tightly. Place onto a serving platter and drizzle a little more olive oil over, a grind of black pepper and some extra herbs.

Watermelon and haloumi

Serves 4 to 6 people

Ingredients

1 fl oz/30 ml olive oil
32 oz/1 kg watermelon, cut into chunks
9 oz/250 g haloumi cheese, sliced ½ in/1 cm thickness
½ Spanish onion, finely sliced (optional)

½ oz/10 g fresh mint leaves
2 tbs parsley, finely chopped
1 lemon

Method

Fry or grill the haloumi on a medium/high heat for 2–3 minutes on each side until golden brown.
   Place the watermelon chunks into a large serving bowl, drizzle with the olive oil, and a good squeeze of lemon and add the herbs and onion (if using). Add the haloumi and using your hands combine gently.

Variations

Watermelon, haloumi with shrimp

24 cooked shrimp (prawns)

Add cooked shrimp to the salad and combine gently.
   If using green shrimp, sauté in 1 fl oz/30 ml olive oil for 2 minutes, or until cooked. Cool and add to the watermelon and haloumi.

Watermelon, haloumi with chicken

4½ oz/125 g shredded cooked chicken or 2 chicken fillets grilled or pan-fried
1 handful baby spinach

Add the baby spinach to the watermelon and haloumi salad. Top the salad with the chicken and combine gently.

Salt cured olives

Olives are the simplest of meze dishes, perfect with fresh crusty bread, this for me is typically Mediterranean. I like to use ripe black olives for salt curing and this method gives the olives a wrinkled appearance. You can preserve as many or as little olives as you desire.

Place the black olives onto some cheesecloth and cover with a layer of coarse rock salt and suspend over a bucket or place into a colander over a bucket. Toss the olives with the salt daily and the juice will begin to drain.

This process should take about two weeks and you will notice that the olives will begin to look wrinkled. You can check if they are ready by tasting to see if the bitterness has gone and the flesh should be dark all the way through.

When they are ready, rinse them well and you can use them straight away in casseroles or salads.

To store your olives simply pour into sterilized jars filled with salty brine and topped with a little olive oil to seal or only olive oil.

Olives can be stored in a cool dark pantry for up to a year in a sealed jar either in the brine or oil.

Baccalà croquettes

Ingredients

Olive oil

32 oz/1 kg salt cod

2½ oz/60 g breadcrumbs

2½ oz/60 g plain flour

Lemon

2 tbs dill, finely chopped

2 tbs parsley, finely chopped

Salt, to taste

Freshly ground black pepper

Method

Prepare the salt cod by removing the skin and cutting it into pieces. Place into a large bowl and cover with cold water. It will need to soak overnight to remove the salt.

Remove the water and drain well. Flake the fish using a fork removing any bones. Place the flaked fish into a bowl with the breadcrumbs, flour and herbs. Add a good squeeze of lemon and season to taste with salt (check to see if it needs it) and pepper. The mixture should be a little soft and not too thick.

In a large frying pan pour enough oil to the depth of ½ in/1 cm and heat. Using a large tablespoon place carefully into the hot oil a spoonful of the baccalà mixture. Fry on both sides until golden brown and allow it to rest on absorbent paper while cooking the remaining mixture.

Serve immediately with the Butter Bean Skordalia (see recipe page 41).

Fava

Serves 4 to 6 people

Ingredients

17½ oz/500 g split yellow peas (fava)
1 fl oz/30 ml olive oil
1 small onion, grated
Salt, to taste
Freshly ground black pepper
2 tbs parsley, finely chopped

Method

Wash the split peas under some cold water in a colander. Add the peas into a large pot of boiling water, about 1¾ pint/1 litre and simmer covered for about 30 minutes.

While this is cooking, sauté in a frying pan the grated onion in the olive oil until soft. Add to the split peas and mix well. Add salt to taste. Simmer for another 30 minutes or until the peas have absorbed all the water.

Remove from heat and either blitz with a hand-held blender or stir rapidly with a wooden spoon until smooth.

Spoon onto a serving dish and drizzle some olive oil, a squeeze of lemon and sprinkle with parsley and a grinding of black pepper.

Butter bean skordalia

Serves 4 to 6 people

Ingredients

2 fl oz/60 ml olive oil
17½ oz/500 g butter beans (canned is fine)
2 fl oz/60 ml lemon juice
4 tbs water
3 cloves garlic, minced
Salt and freshly ground pepper, to taste

Method

Place the drained butter beans in a blender with the lemon juice, water, garlic and salt and pepper to taste. Blend until it resembles a thick paste then slowly drizzle the olive oil until smooth and silky. You may need to use more than 2 fl oz/60 ml of olive oil. Check for seasoning, adding more if needed then place into a bowl, cover and refrigerate until needed. Alternatively, serve immediately.

Hummus

Serves 4 to 6 people

Ingredients

9 oz/250 g chickpeas (soaked overnight)

½ tsp bicarbonate of soda

2½ oz/60 g tahini paste

3 tbs lemon juice

2 fl oz/60 ml olive oil

2 garlic cloves, finely diced

1 tsp sweet paprika, to serve

2 tbs parsley, finely chopped for serving

Salt, to taste

Freshly ground black pepper

Method

Soak the chickpeas in water with the bicarbonate of soda overnight. Drain and rinse well. Place the chickpeas in a large pot of water, cover and bring to the boil and cook until very soft. This should take about 40–50 minutes.

Drain the chickpeas and place them into a food processor and process until all mashed. While still processing add tahini paste, garlic, lemon juice and slowly drizzle the olive oil in creating a smooth paste.

Season to taste.

Pour the hummus into a serving bowl and chill in the refrigerator for an hour before serving. Serve with a drizzle of olive oil and a sprinkling of sweet paprika and parsley.

Chickpea fritters

Serves 4 to 6 people

Ingredients

1 fl oz/30 ml olive oil, plus extra for frying

17½ oz/500 g chickpeas (soaked overnight in salted water, 1 tbs salt)

1 onion, grated

1 tbs mint, finely chopped

1 tbs dill, finely chopped

5 oz/150 g plain flour

2 large ripe tomatoes, grated

½ tsp sweet paprika

Salt, to taste

Freshly ground black pepper

Lemon juice to serve

Method

Soak the chickpeas in salted water overnight. Drain and wash the chickpeas well, then using a food processor or wooden spoon mix until it resembles a paste. Add the onion, herbs, tomato, paprika and oil and season well. Add the flour slowly mixing well as you go until the mixture looks like a thick paste. Cover and place in the refrigerator for about one hour to rest.

Heat extra olive oil in a frying pan and add large tablespoons of the chickpea mixture, cooking on all sides until golden, about 8–10 minutes. Do not overcrowd the frying pan. Place cooked fritters on absorbent paper while cooking the rest of the mixture. Arrange fritters on a serving platter and squeeze over a little lemon juice and serve at room temperature.

Spicy Feta dip (tirokafteri)

Serves 4 to 6 people

Ingredients

9 oz/250 g feta cheese
4 fl oz/120 ml Greek yogurt
1 tbs olive oil
1 tsp red wine vinegar
*1 roasted red pepper, seeded and minced (can be store
  bought)*
Chilli flakes (optional)

Method

In a large bowl, mash the feta cheese together with the yogurt using a fork. Add the olive oil and vinegar and mix well. Add the roasted red pepper and chilli flakes if you want more heat, and combine.

   Cover and leave in the refrigerator for at least one hour before serving.

Fried eggplant with tzatziki

Serves 4 to 6 people

Ingredients

2 or 3 eggplant (aubergines)
Olive oil
Plain four, for coating
Salt, to taste
Freshly ground black pepper

Method

Prepare the eggplant by slicing lengthways in half then into half circle slices.
   Place some plain flour, about 5 oz/150 g, into a bowl. Pour some cold water into another bowl.
   Pour some olive oil into a frying pan, about ½ in/1 cm deep. Dip the eggplant slices into the flour, then into the water and back into the flour, shaking off any excess as you go. Carefully place into the olive oil and fry, turning once until golden.
   Carefully remove from oil and place on absorbent paper while cooking. Arrange onto a serving platter when all cooked and season with salt and pepper. Serve with tzatziki.

Soups

Comforting and nourishing soups are enjoyed in the cooler weather and some even in the summer months. This section features the delicious chicken avgolemono and many other traditional hearty soups where pulses are the main ingredients. Enjoy them whatever the season.

Vegetable Soup

Serves 4 to 6 people

Ingredients

1 large red onion, finely diced

4 pints/2 l of water (if you prefer you can use some vegetable stock)

Salt, to taste

Freshly ground black pepper, to taste

3½ ml/100 ml olive oil

3 small tomatoes, peeled, seeded and diced

2 heaped tbs parsley, finely chopped

2 zucchini (courgettes), sliced

2 carrots, diced

1 celery stalk, sliced

5 oz/150 g fresh or frozen green peas

1½ oz/40 g finely chopped lettuce leaves (you can use spinach, cabbage, celery leaves, fennel or other seasonal greens that you prefer)

3½ oz/100 g tiny pasta (optional)

Method

Heat the olive oil in a large pot and sauté the onions until soft. Add the prepared vegetables and mix well so they are covered in olive oil. Pour in the water (or stock) and bring to the boil. Cover and simmer on a low heat for 30 minutes or until the vegetables are cooked. Add the pasta, if using, after 20 minutes and simmer for a further 10 minutes. Season to taste and sprinkle with parsley before serving.

Serve hot with fresh crusty bread and feta cheese.

Avgolemono soup

Ingredients

750 g chicken pieces (thighs, legs and wings are
  good for stock)
5½ oz/160 g short grain rice
Salt, to taste
Freshly ground black pepper
Egg and lemon sauce (see recipe page 182)

Method

Place the chicken pieces in a large pot of water, about 2½ pints/1½ litres. Bring to boil and simmer until the chicken is cooked and tender. Remove the chicken and strain the stock. You should have about 1¾ pints/1 litre of stock.

Bring the stock back to the boil and add the rice. Simmer for about 10–12 minutes or until rice is tender. Turn off the heat. Season to taste.

Add the prepared egg and lemon sauce slowly to the soup. You can shred the cooked chicken and return to the soup or serve it as an accompaniment.

Serve immediately.

Lentil soup with risoni

Ingredients

1 onion, finely diced

2 cloves garlic, finely diced

1 stick celery, sliced

4 large tomatoes peeled and quartered

7 oz/200 g brown lentils

1 bay leaf

1 heaped tbs parsley, chopped

1 heaped tbs mint, finely chopped

Salt, to taste

Ground black pepper, to taste

3½ fl oz/100 ml olive oil plus a little extra for serving

2 tbs red wine vinegar

3 oz/80 g risoni

4 pints/2 l water

Method

Heat the olive oil in a large pot and sauté the onions until soft. Add the garlic, peeled and quartered tomatoes and celery. Wash the lentils and add to the pot, stirring well so the lentils are covered with the oil.

Pour in the water, add the bay leaf and bring to the boil. Simmer on a low heat until the lentils are al dente. Add the risoni and cook for a further 10 minutes or until the risoni is done.

Remove the bay leaf and season with salt and pepper. Add the parsley, mint and vinegar and drizzle with a little olive oil before serving.

Serve hot.

Vegetables & Salads

Vegetables and salads are eaten every day and most meals are centred round fresh, seasonal vegetables, they are one of the main ingredients in the Greek Mediterranean cuisine.

Oven roasted tomatoes and peppers salad

Serves 4 to 6 people

Ingredients

9 oz/250 g tomatoes
9 oz/250 g red pepper (capsicum)
3½ oz/100 ml olive oil
Salt, to taste
Freshly ground black pepper, to taste
2 heaped tbs fresh thyme, chopped
2 heaped tbs fresh parsley, chopped

Method

Prepare the tomatoes and red pepper by cutting in half and removing seeds, then chopping into large chunks.

Place in a bowl and pour over the olive oil, thyme, parsley, salt and pepper and mix carefully to combine.

Pour out onto a baking dish and bake in a preheated oven at 350°F/180°C for 30–40 minutes or until cooked.

Serve at room temperature or cold with fresh crusty bread and feta cheese.

This is also lovely stirred through some pasta as a sauce.

Fruit salad with mint and honey yogurt

Serves 4 to 6 people

Ingredients

2 peaches

4 apricots

2 nectarines

Punnet of strawberries

½ small watermelon

16 fl oz/480 ml Greek yogurt

4 fl oz/120 ml thyme honey

1 tsp vanilla extract

Small bunch of mint leaves

4½ oz/120 g roasted almonds or pistachios

Method

In a medium bowl place the yogurt, honey and vanilla extract. Mix well and set aside.

Prepare the fruit by removing the stones and cutting the stone fruits into quarters and cutting the watermelon into chunks. Place all the fruit into a large serving bowl and sprinkle with the mint leaves and nuts.

Serve with the honey yogurt on the side.

Greek salad with purslane

Serves 4 to 6 people

Ingredients

3 tomatoes cut into wedges

1 red onion, peeled and sliced

1 cucumber, sliced

1 green pepper (capsicum), sliced

1 handful of purslane (you can use rocket instead if you
  cannot get a hold of purslane)

2 tbs chopped dill

2 tbs chopped parsley

2 tbs chopped mint

1 tbs dried oregano

3½ oz/100 g kalamata olives

Salt, to taste

2 fl oz/60 ml olive oil

½ fl oz/20 ml red wine vinegar

4½ oz/120 g feta cheese, cubed or crumbled

Method

Arrange the tomatoes, onions, cucumber, pepper, purslane and herbs in a serving bowl. Mix gently and top with olives and feta cheese.

Pour the olive oil, vinegar, oregano and seasonings into a jar, close the lid and shake until all the ingredients are blended.

Drizzle over the salad and serve.

Bulgar wheat salad

Serves 4 to 6 people

Ingredients

1 fl oz/30 ml olive oil

1 small red onion, finely diced

7 oz/200 g bulgar wheat

17 fl oz/500 ml water

Salt, to taste

Freshly ground black pepper, to taste

Seeds of one pomegranate

3½ oz/100 g raisins or currants

2 tbs fresh mint, finely chopped

2 tbs fresh parsley, finely chopped

2½ oz/60 g pumpkin seeds

Rind of one orange

Lemon

Method

Place the bulgar wheat in a bowl and pour over enough boiling water to cover. Cover the bowl and leave for about 20 minutes.

Put the bulgar wheat in a serving dish and add the onion, pomegranate seeds, herbs, pumpkin seeds and orange rind. Combine gently and drizzle with olive oil and squeeze ½ lemon over. Season to taste.

Braised dandelion

Ingredients

1 small bunch dandelion greens (remove tough stems)
2 fl oz/60 ml olive oil
Juice of ½ lemon
Salt, to taste
Freshly ground black pepper, to taste

Method

Wash the dandelion leaves well and remove any tough stems.

Cook the greens in a large pot of salted water until tender, about 6–8 minutes.

Drain the greens, squeeze dry and place in a bowl.

Drizzle the olive oil over and the lemon juice, season with salt and pepper and serve at room temperature.

Green beans and tomato salad

Ingredients

14 oz/400 g green beans

4 large ripe tomatoes, chopped

1 tsp dried oregano

1 red onion, peeled and sliced

2 tbs parsley, finely chopped

2 tbs mint, finely chopped

2 tbs dill, finely chopped

Salt, to taste

Fresh ground black pepper, to taste

Chunks of day old bread (optional)

Feta, to serve

Olives, to serve

4 fl oz/120 ml olive oil

2 fl oz/60 ml red wine vinegar

Method

Place the beans into a pot of salted boiling water for about 2–3 minutes. Drain and place the beans in a pot of cold water to stop the cooking process and keep the color. Drain well and dry on some paper toweling.

Transfer the beans to a serving dish and add the tomatoes, onion, herbs and season to taste. Combine gently and drizzle over the olive oil and red wine vinegar. Add the bread (optional) and using your hands gently combine all the ingredients.

Perfect on its own with fresh crusty bread, feta and olives or with any meat, fish or poultry.

Spinach salad with fresh figs and goat's cheese

Serves 4 to 6 people

Ingredients

5 oz/150 g baby spinach leaves

2 tbs olive oil

1 tbs balsamic or red wine vinegar

2 oz/50 g pumpkin seeds

3½ oz/100 g soft goat's cheese

2 oz/50 g sultanas

6 fresh ripe figs, quartered

Salt, to taste

Freshly ground black pepper

Method

In a large bowl pour in the olive oil and vinegar and mix well. Place the spinach leaves in the dressing and combine using your hands gently.

Take the leaves out of the dressing and place onto a serving dish. Place the quartered figs onto the spinach and sprinkle with crumbled goat's cheese, sultanas and pumpkin seeds.

Drizzle a little more olive oil over and season to taste.

Cabbage and iceberg salad

Serves 4 to 6 people

Ingredients

¼ cabbage, shredded finely
1 small iceberg lettuce, chopped
2 oz/50 g rocket
1 small red pepper (capsicum), diced
1 small yellow pepper (capsicum), diced
6–8 roma tomatoes, cut in half and quartered

3½ oz/100 g corn kernels
2 fl oz/60 ml olive oil
1 fl oz/30 ml lemon juice
Zest of one lemon
Salt, to taste
Freshly ground black pepper

Method

Pour the olive oil and lemon juice into a jar and shake well to combine. Pour into a large bowl.

Place the cabbage, lettuce, rocket, pepper, tomatoes and corn on to the dressing and using your hands gently combine. Season to taste and finish off with a sprinkling of lemon zest and a drizzle of extra olive oil.

Spinach salad with fruits and nuts

Serves 4 to 6 people

Ingredients

5 oz/150 g baby spinach leaves

1 banana, sliced

1 apple, sliced

3½ oz/100 g grapes

2 peaches, sliced

1 tbs sesame seeds

3½ oz/100 g walnuts

2 tbs olive oil

1 tbs balsamic or red wine vinegar

Salt, to taste

Freshly ground black pepper

Fresh mint leaves for serving

Method

In a large bowl mix the olive oil and vinegar well. Add the spinach and combine, coating all the leaves with dressing using your hands. Place the spinach leaves onto a serving platter and add the banana, apples and peaches, combining gently. Sprinkle with the sesame seeds, walnuts, some fresh mint leaves and a little extra olive oil. Season to taste.

Stuffed onions

Serves 4 to 6 people

Ingredients

7 red onions
3½ fl oz/100 ml olive oil
5 oz/150 g minced beef
3½ oz/100 g rice
3 heaped tbs parsley, finely chopped
4 large ripe tomatoes, grated

Salt, to taste
Freshly ground black pepper
3½ oz/100 g pine nuts
3½ oz/100 g sultanas
1 lemon

Method

This is also lovely made without the mince, simply leave out the mince and increase the quantity of rice to 7 oz/200 g.

Peel 6 of the onions and slice lengthways but not all the way through, leaving the onion connected at the base. Place them in a large saucepan of boiling water carefully and cook for about 10–12 minutes or until tender. Drain and put aside to cool.

In a frying pan heat the olive oil and sauté the remaining onion (finely diced) until soft. Add the mince, rice, tomatoes, parsley, pine nuts and sultanas. Season to taste.

Preheat oven at 350°F/180°C.

When the onions are cool enough to handle, carefully remove the leaves. Place a leaf into the palm of your hand and put a spoonful of the mixture into it and roll, (similar to making dolmades). Continue until all the leaves have been filled and rolled and placing them into a baking dish packed tightly so they do not unroll. Any leaves that are too small to roll can be added to the baking tray together with any mixture that may be left over. Drizzle olive oil over the onions and pour enough water over to come halfway up the onions, but not covering them. Place a plate on top so they stay in place and bake for about 30–40 minutes or until cooked and golden.

Serve with fresh crusty bread.

Wild greens salad with pomegranate

Serves 4 to 6 people

Ingredients

14 oz/400 g salad greens (spinach, endive, radicchio,
   chicory, chard, arugula (rocket))

7 oz/200 g pomegranate seeds

2 fl oz/60 ml olive oil

1 tbs honey

1 tsp pomegranate molasses

1 fl oz/30 ml red wine vinegar

1 fennel bulb, finely sliced

1 orange, remove the skin and pith and cut into segments,

Salt, to taste

Freshly ground pepper

1½ oz/40 g toasted pine nuts

Method

Arrange the salad greens onto a serving platter. Add the fennel and orange segments.

Place the olive oil, vinegar, honey, pomegranate molasses and seasonings into a jar, cover tightly and shake until all the ingredients are blended.

Sprinkle pomegranate seeds and pine nuts over and drizzle with the dressing to serve.

Fried green peppers

Serves 4 to 6 people

Ingredients

8 sweet green peppers
2 fl oz/60 ml olive oil
Salt, to taste
1 tbs dried oregano

Method

Slice the tops halfway, keeping peppers attached and remove the seeds.

In a frying pan heat the olive oil and add the peppers. Sauté on a high heat turning gently so they are browned on all sides. Remove when cooked and serve with a sprinkling of oregano and salt.

Serve with some fresh bread and feta cheese.

Green salad with berries

Ingredients

14 oz/400 g green salad leaves (arugula (rocket), radicchio
   and shredded red cabbage)

1 mango, cut into slices

1 avocado, cut in slices

7 oz/200 g pomegranate seeds

14 oz/400 g mixed berries (blueberries, raspberries, black-
   berries)

Dressing

2 fl oz/60 ml olive oil

1 fl oz/30 ml balsamic vinegar

1 tbs honey

1 tsp Dijon mustard

Method

Place all the washed and dried salad leaves onto a serving platter. Top with the mango, avocado, mixed berries and pomegranate seeds.

Place all the ingredients for the dressing in a jar, cover tightly and shake until all blended well.

Drizzle dressing on the salad and serve.

Bulgar and parsley salad

Serves 4 to 6 people

Ingredients

3 oz/75 g bulgar wheat

3½ oz/100 g feta

3½ fl oz/100 ml olive oil

3 oz/75 g finely chopped fresh parsley

¾ oz/20 g finely chopped mint leaves

Juice of one lemon

2 large tomatoes, diced

1 small red onion, finely diced

Seeds of one pomegranate (optional)

Salt, to taste

Freshly ground black pepper

Method

Soak the bulgar wheat in boiling water for about 1 minute. Drain well, dry and place in a large bowl.

Prepare the tomatoes, slicing and dicing each slice. Add the tomato, onion, mint and parsley to the bulgar.

Drizzle over the olive oil; squeeze the lemon and season with salt and pepper to taste. Sprinkle with the pomegranate seeds.

Green salad with spring onions

Ingredients

9 oz/250 g mixed lettuce (butter, cos, endive)

4 scallions (spring onions), sliced thinly

2 tbs capers, whole

1 heaped tbs dill, finely chopped

2 fl oz/60 ml olive oil

Juice and zest of one lemon

Salt, to taste

Freshly ground black pepper

Method

Wash, drain and dry the lettuce and place in a bowl.

In a large bowl pour the olive oil, lemon juice and zest and mix well. Season to taste. Place the lettuce leaves and scallions into the dressing and combine gently using your hands. Arrange onto a serving dish and sprinkle with the capers and dill.

Drizzle a little more olive oil before serving.

Kastro
Oia Houses

Potato salad

Ingredients

32 oz/1 kg potatoes

5 fl oz/150 ml olive oil

Juice and zest of 2 lemons

Salt, to taste

Freshly ground black pepper

1 bunch of scallions (spring onions), finely chopped

3 heaped tbs parsley, finely chopped

2 oz/50 g kalamata olives (optional)

2 tbs capers (optional)

Method

Boil the potatoes whole in a large pot of water until tender. Remove carefully from the water and allow them to cool. Once the potatoes are cool enough to handle remove the skins and chop into chunks.

Place the potatoes into a serving bowl and add the olive oil, lemon juice and rind, scallions, parsley, capers and olives (if using) and season to taste. Combine gently.

Serve at room temperature or cold.

Green beans and amaranth (vlita) casserole

Serves 4 to 6 people

Ingredients

32 oz/1 kg green beans, trimmed

9 oz/250 g amaranth (you could also use dandelion
  or spinach) washed and roughly chopped

4 potatoes, peeled and cut into chunks

3½ fl oz/100 ml olive oil

1 onion, finely diced

4 large ripe tomatoes, grated

2 cloves garlic, finely diced

2 heaped tbs parsley, finely chopped

1 tbs mint leaves, finely chopped

1 tbs dill, finely chopped

Salt, to taste

Freshly ground black pepper

Method

In a large casserole pot heat the olive oil and sauté the onions until soft. Add the garlic and tomatoes and 8 fl oz/240 ml of water. Allow to simmer for 4–5 minutes. Add the green beans and simmer for a further 10 minutes. Add the potatoes, amaranth leaves and herbs. Season to taste and continue cooking for a further 10–15 minutes or until all the vegetables are tender.

Serve hot or at room temperature with fresh crusty bread and some feta cheese.

Amaranth (vlita) and zucchini

Serves 4 to 6 people

I loved the way my mother would grate her tomatoes when making casseroles and sauces. She would simply cut the tomato in half, hold one half in the palm of her hand, cut side facing out and grate against a grater until she was left with just the tomato skin against her palm and a bowl full of gorgeous tomato puree.

Ingredients

1 bunch amaranth leaves (approx. 32 oz/1 kg)
   roughly chopped
6 small zucchini (courgettes)
4 fl oz/120 ml olive oil
2 cloves garlic, finely diced
1 brown onion, finely diced

4–6 ripe tomatoes, grated
Salt, to taste
Freshly ground black pepper
1 lemon
Parsley for serving

Method

Prepare the amaranth leaves by washing well under cold water and chop roughly. Slice the zucchini into small discs.

In a large pot heat the olive oil and sauté the onions until soft, add the garlic and grated tomato, combine well and allow to simmer on a low heat for 4–5 minutes. Add the sliced zucchini and continue cooking for a further 5 minutes. Add the amaranth leaves and combine gently. You can add a little water if it looks too dry, 4 fl oz/120 ml should be enough.

Simmer for 10–12 minutes or until the vegetables are tender. Shake the pot a little instead of mixing to keep vegetables whole.

Season to taste. Sprinkle with parsley and a squeeze of lemon before serving.

Artichoke and bean salad

Serves 4 to 6 people

Ingredients

3½ fl oz/100 ml olive oil

4 artichoke hearts

3½ oz/100 g freshly shelled broad beans

3½ oz/100 g green beans, trimmed

2 scallions (spring onions), sliced

1 tbs parsley, finely chopped

2 tbs dill, finely chopped

Salt, to taste

Freshly ground black pepper

Lemon

Method

In a saucepan heat the olive oil and sauté the scallions until soft. Add the artichoke hearts, broad beans and green beans. Add about 8 fl oz/240 ml of water, season to taste and add the herbs. Simmer for about 30 minutes or until the vegetables are cooked.

Serve salad at room temperature with an extra drizzle of olive oil and a squeeze of lemon.

Olive oil roasted vegetables

Serves 4 to 6 people

Ingredients

5 fl oz/150 ml olive oil

2 eggplants (aubergines)

3 zucchini (courgette)

2 carrots

6 potatoes

2 red onions

1 green pepper (capsicum)

1 red pepper (capsicum)

4 tomatoes, grated

2 heaped tbs chopped parsley

Salt, to taste

Freshly ground black pepper

1 tbs dried oregano

Method

Preheat the oven at 350°F/180°C. Cut the eggplant into chunks, sprinkle with salt and allow it to sit in a colander for 30 minutes. Rinse and dry well.

Place all the prepared vegetables into a large baking dish and pour over the olive oil. Add the parsley, oregano, season with salt and pepper and combine gently. Add 4 fl oz/120 ml water and cover with foil. Bake for about 2 hours.

Remove foil and bake for a further 30 minutes or until vegetables are cooked through and golden.

Variations

Olive oil roasted vegetables with salmon or fish fillets

Half way through roasting the vegetables you can top with salmon fillets, snapper fillets or other fish that you prefer.

Drizzle the fish with a little olive oil and a sprinkling of salt. Continue cooking until the vegetables are tender and fish is cooked through.

Braised eggplant and tomato

Ingredients

3½ fl oz/100 ml olive oil

3 eggplant (aubergines), cut into chunks

1 onion, finely chopped

6 large ripe tomatoes, cut into chunks

2 heaped tbs parsley, finely chopped

1 tsp dried oregano

2 cloves garlic, finely diced

2 tbs red wine vinegar

1 tbs capers

3 oz/75 g pitted kalamata olives

4 potatoes, cut into chunks (optional)

Salt, to taste

Freshly ground black pepper

Method

In a large casserole dish heat the olive oil and sauté the onion, garlic and eggplant chunks for a few minutes.

Add the tomatoes, red wine vinegar, potatoes and 16 fl oz/480 ml of water. Simmer for 20 minutes. Add the herbs, capers, kalamata olives and season to taste. Continue cooking for a further 5–10 minutes or until vegetables are tender.

Serve hot or at room temperature with fresh crusty bread.

Purslane and herb salad

Ingredients

1 oz/25 g purslane
1 oz/25 g arugula (rocket)
1½ oz/40 g pumpkin seeds
1½ oz/40 g sunflower seeds
¾ oz/20 g sesame seeds

(toast the seeds lightly in a frying pan with 1 tbs of olive oil)
2 fl oz/60 ml olive oil
1 fl oz/30 ml lemon juice
Salt, to taste
Freshly ground black pepper

Method

Pour the olive oil, lemon juice and seasonings into a jar, close tightly and shake until all combined.

Arrange the purslane and rocket onto a serving platter. Scatter with the seeds and drizzle the salad dressing over. Combine gently.

Serve immediately.

Roasted potatoes in olive oil and paprika

Serves 4 to 6 people

Ingredients

32 oz/1 kg potatoes
3½ fl oz/100 ml olive oil
2 ripe tomatoes, grated
1 tbs dried oregano
1 tbs sweet paprika
Salt, to taste
Freshly ground black pepper

Method

Peel and slice the potatoes into rounds ½ in/1 cm thickness. Place into a large bowl and add the olive oil, dried oregano, sweet paprika, grated tomato, salt and pepper and gently combine using your hands.

Pour into a baking dish and arrange potatoes evenly. Add 4 fl oz/120 ml water and bake in a preheated oven at 350°F/180°C for about 40 minutes or until the potatoes are cooked. You can add a little more water if it is looking too dry.

Cretan rusk salad (dakos)

Serves 4 to 6 people

Ingredients

4½ oz/120 g Cretan barley rusks (or other rusks)

2 fl oz/60 ml olive oil

1 fl oz/30 ml balsamic vinegar

5 large tomatoes, seeded and diced

½ red onion, diced

3½ oz/100 g feta cheese, crumbled

1 oz/30 g kalamata olives, pitted and sliced

1 heaped tbs parsley, finely chopped

½ tsp dried oregano

Salt, to taste

Freshly ground black pepper

Method

Place the rusks (broken into chunks) onto a serving platter.

In a large bowl place the tomato, onion, olive oil, oregano, balsamic vinegar and season to taste. Combine gently and spoon the mixture over the rusks. Crumble the feta over the salad and sprinkle the olives and parsley and allow to rest for a few minutes before serving.

Serve with an extra drizzle of olive oil.

Vegetable bake with béchamel

Serves 4 to 6 people

Ingredients

5 fl oz/150 ml olive oil

4 large eggplant (aubergines), sliced

2 large potatoes, peeled and sliced

6 zucchini (courgettes), sliced

1 onion, finely chopped or grated

2 cloves garlic, minced

6 tomatoes, peeled, seeded and diced

3 heaped tbs parsley, finely chopped

2 heaped tbs dill, finely chopped

1 tsp oregano

½ tsp sugar

Salt, to taste

Freshly ground black pepper

7 oz/200 g feta cheese

Béchamel sauce (see recipe page 183)

Method

Preheat oven to 400°F/200°C. Trim and slice the eggplant. Sprinkle with a little salt and leave to drain for one hour. Rinse and pat dry with paper towels.

Slice the zucchini and put aside. Prepare the potatoes and put into a large bowl of water.

In a large frying pan heat half the oil. Remove the potatoes from the water; drain and pat dry with paper towels. Fry the potatoes until golden brown. Remove and place onto some kitchen paper to absorb any excess oil. Using the same oil, add the eggplants and zucchini, frying for 3–4 minutes on each side, or until golden. Remove and place onto some absorbent paper to remove any excess oil.

Pour the remaining oil into a saucepan and heat. Add the onion and cook until soft. Add the garlic, sugar and tomatoes and simmer for 10–12 minutes, until it thickens and resembles a sauce. Add the herbs and season to taste.

Make the béchamel sauce.

In a large, lightly oiled baking dish place the potatoes; cover with the eggplant and on top with the zucchini. Crumble the feta cheese over the vegetables and pour over the tomato sauce. Top with the béchamel sauce and bake in the oven for about 1 hour or until golden brown.

Serve hot or at room temperature.

Beetroot, purslane and herb salad

Serves 4 to 6 people

Ingredients

4 large beetroots, boiled, peeled and cut into chunks

2 oz/50 g purslane leaves (you can use arugula (rocket)
  if you prefer)

One handful of mint leaves

Dressing

2 fl oz/60 ml olive oil

1 fl oz/30 ml red wine vinegar

1 tsp sugar

Juice of ½ orange

Orange zest

Salt, to taste

Method

Place the beetroot in a serving bowl. Wash and dry the purslane and mint leaves and add to the beetroot.

Place all the ingredients for the dressing in a jar and shake or in a bowl and whisk for a couple of minutes until combined.

Drizzle the dressing over the salad and mix gently. Serve.

Pies and bread

The smell of pies filled with delicious fillings and gorgeous generous breads permeate kitchens throughout providing warmth, comfort and generosity. Gorgeous pies are a staple and are perfect served on a meze plate or as a light lunch with a salad.

Rustic homemade filo

Makes 2 pies

Ingredients

17½ oz/500 g baker's flour
1 tsp sugar
2 tsp salt
2 tsp baking powder
2 tbs olive oil
1 tbs vinegar
8 fl oz/240 ml warm water

Method

Sift the flour and place into a large mixing bowl with the salt, sugar and baking powder. Make a well in the centre and pour in the olive oil, vinegar and warm water. Mix the flour into the liquid mixture slowly, if necessary add more water.

Knead the mixture into a soft and elastic dough. Make a ball with the dough, leave in the bowl, cover with a cloth and allow it to rest for at least an hour.

When ready to use divide the dough into small balls and roll out into sheets using a long thin rolling pin. Keep rolling all directions until you have made a large round very fine sheet. When using these sheets brush with a little melted butter and olive oil between sheets.

To make pita filo which separates during baking, stack three or four balls of dough on each other brushed with a little melted butter together with olive oil. Roll this stack into a sheet.

They are now ready for your delicious fillings.

Zucchini, Swiss chard and feta pie

Serves 4 to 6 people

Ingredients

3½ fl oz/100 ml olive oil

32 oz/1 kg zucchini

17½ oz/500 g Swiss chard (you can use spinach if
  you prefer)

1 onion, finely diced

7 oz/200 g feta cheese crumbled (you can use a
  combination of feta and ricotta if you prefer)

3 eggs

2 heaped tbs parsley, finely chopped

2 heaped tbs mint leaves, finely chopped

2 heaped tbs dill, finely chopped

1 tsp dried oregano

Salt, to taste

Freshly ground black pepper

1 quantity filo pastry (you can make your own or store
  bought)

Method

Preheat oven to 350°F/180°C. Prepare the filling by grating the zucchini, sprinkle with a little salt and mix well. Transfer to a colander to drain for about one hour. Take the zucchini mixture and squeeze out any excess liquid and place in a large bowl. Wash the chard well, dry and chop roughly.

In a frying pan heat about 1 fl oz/30 ml of olive oil, add the onion and chard and fry for a few minutes until soft. Add the chard mixture, feta cheese, eggs and herbs to the zucchini. Combine well and season to taste.

Prepare a large baking dish brushing it with some olive oil. Lay a filo pastry sheet into the baking dish and brush with the olive oil. Continue this with half the filo pastry, brushing each sheet as you go. Spread the filling into the dish and top with the remaining filo sheets, brushing with the oil again as you go. Brush the top sheet well and score the pastry in a few places.

Sprinkle with a little water before placing into oven. Bake for an hour, or until pastry is golden and crispy.

Serve at room temperature.

Wild greens pie

Serves 4 to 6 people

Ingredients

3½ fl oz/100 ml olive oil

32 oz/1 kg wild greens (use a combination of Swiss chard, dandelion leaves, spinach and curly endive)

2 heaped tbs parsley, finely chopped

2 heaped tbs dill, finely chopped

6 scallions (spring onions), finely sliced

9 oz/250 g feta, crumbled

3½ oz/100 g ricotta, crumbled

2 eggs

Lemon zest of ½ lemon

1 quantity of filo pastry (homemade or store bought)

Method

Prepare the wild greens by rinsing under cold water and leave to drain in a colander. Chop the wild greens roughly and place in a large bowl. Add the herbs, scallions, feta, ricotta, eggs and lemon zest.

Preheat the oven at 350°F/180°C. Prepare a large baking dish brushing it with some olive oil.

Lay a filo pastry sheet into the baking dish and brush with the olive oil. Continue this with half the filo pastry, (approximately 6–8 sheets) brushing each sheet as you go. Spread the wild greens filling into the dish and top with the remaining filo sheets, brushing with the oil again as you go. Brush the top sheet well and score the pastry in a few places.

Sprinkle with a little water before placing into oven. Bake for an hour or until pastry is golden and crispy.

Serve at room temperature.

Olive oil flatbread

Serves 4 to 6 people

Ingredients

2 fl oz/60 ml olive oil

1 oz/30 g fresh yeast or ½ oz/7 g dry yeast

10 fl oz/300 ml warm water

1 tbs sugar

14 oz/400 g plain bread flour

1 tsp salt

1 tbs sesame or poppy seeds

Oregano or rosemary (optional)

Method

In a medium bowl crumble the fresh yeast or scatter the dry yeast, add the sugar and add the warm water. Mix well, cover with a tea towel and allow to rest for 10 minutes, or until it begins to bubble. Add the flour, salt and olive oil mixing with a wooden spoon until all combined and then continue mixing with your hands until it resembles a soft dough.

Pour the dough out onto a working bench and knead until it is smooth and elastic. You can also use an electric mixer with a dough hook if you prefer.

Put the dough back into a clean bowl and cover with cling wrap and a tea towel. Allow it to sit for about an hour for the yeast to activate and the dough to rise.

Preheat the oven to 400°C/200°C.

Roll out the dough on a lightly floured working bench, ½ in/1 cm thickness, and place onto a lightly oiled baking tray. Brush the dough with a little water and sprinkle with the seeds or salt. You may like to sprinkle with some herbs instead. I like oregano or rosemary.

Make indentations with your fingers if you want all over the dough.

Bake for about 45 minutes or until the dough is cooked through. Remove from the oven, allow to cool a little and serve warm.

Olive flatbread

Serves 4 to 6 people

Ingredients

3½ oz/100 g kalamata olives, drained, pitted and halved
1 tsp dried oregano
Salt, to taste
Olive oil

Method

For the dough follow the recipe for the olive oil flatbread (page 125).

Roll out the dough and place into a lightly oiled baking tray. Brush the top of the dough with a little olive oil and press the olives into the dough. Sprinkle with oregano and some salt to taste.
   Bake for about 45 minutes or until the dough is cooked through.
   Remove from the oven, allow to cool a little and serve warm.

Tomato and onion flatbread

Serves 4 to 6 people

Ingredients

2 large onions, finely sliced
2 large tomatoes, seeded and chopped into chunks
1 tsp dried oregano
½ tsp dried thyme
Salt, to taste
Freshly ground black pepper
2 fl oz/60 ml olive oil

Method

For the dough follow the recipe for the olive oil flatbread (page 125).

Heat the olive oil in a large frying pan and add the onions. Cook for about 5–6 minutes or until soft. Add the tomatoes and continue cooking for a further 5 minutes. Remove from heat and spread the mixture evenly over the prepared dough in the baking dish. Sprinkle with the oregano, thyme, salt and pepper to taste.

Bake for about 45 minutes or until the dough is cooked through.

Remove from the oven, allow to cool a little and serve warm.

Chicken filo pie

Serves 4 to 6 people

Ingredients

3½ fl oz/100 ml olive oil

1 lb/440 g cooked chicken, shredded

1 onion, finely diced

1 leek, white part only sliced

1 tbs parsley, finely chopped

1 tbs mint, finely chopped

3½ oz/100 g golden raisins

2 eggs, lightly beaten

1 tsp ground cinnamon

1 tsp ground nutmeg

3½ oz/100 g kefalotyri, grated (or parmesan)

Method

In a large frying pan heat half the olive oil and sauté the onion and leek until soft. Add the chicken and spices and cook for a further 5 minutes on a low heat. Turn off the heat and allow to cool. Add the remaining olive oil, herbs, raisins, cheese and eggs. Combine well and season to taste.

Preheat the oven at 350°F/180°C. Prepare a large baking dish brushing it with some olive oil.

Lay a filo pastry sheet into the baking dish and brush with the olive oil. Continue this with half the filo pastry, (approximately 6–8 sheets) brushing each sheet as you go. Spread the chicken filling into the dish and top with the remaining filo sheets, brushing with the oil again as you go. Brush the top sheet well and score the pastry in a few places.

Sprinkle with a little water before placing into oven. Bake for an hour or until pastry is golden and crispy.

Serve at room temperature.

Seafood

Fish is eaten at least twice a week. The simplest and most easily prepared, are fast grilled or fried seafood which are mostly offered as mezedes, nutritious soups to the more substantial casseroles served with potatoes or pasta.

Stuffed tomatoes with calamari, rice and herbs

Serves 4 to 6 people

Ingredients

8 tomatoes
3½ fl oz/100 ml olive oil
1 small brown onion, finely diced
1 clove garlic, finely diced
7 oz/200 g risotto rice
17½ oz/500 g calamari, cut into small pieces

1 tbs parsley, finely chopped
2½ oz/60 g pine nuts
Salt, to taste
Freshly ground pepper, to taste
16 fl oz/480 ml water

Method

Preheat the oven to 350°F/180°C. Prepare the tomatoes by washing them and slicing the tops off. Carefully scoop out the flesh using a teaspoon. Remove the seeds, chop finely and set aside to use in the filling later.

Heat the olive oil in a pan and sauté the onions until softened. Add the garlic, risotto rice and stir well to coat the rice with the oil. Add the tomato flesh and water and simmer for about 15 minutes or until the rice is tender. Add the diced calamari and cook for a few minutes. Add the pine nuts, herbs and season to taste. Spoon mixture into the prepared tomatoes, put lids on and arrange in a baking dish, drizzle with some olive oil and add 8 fl oz/240 ml of water into the dish. Bake in the preheated oven for approximately 35 minutes or until cooked.

Serve hot or at room temperature with fresh crusty bread.

Calamari stifado with risoni

Serves 4 to 6 people

Ingredients

32 oz/1 kg calamari, cleaned and cut into pieces
3½ fl oz/100 ml olive oil
3½ fl oz/100 ml white wine
12 small (pearl) onions, peeled and left whole
2 bay leaves
10 cloves
Zest of one orange

Pinch of cinnamon
4 large ripe tomatoes, grated
Salt, to taste
Ground black pepper, to taste
9 oz/250 g risoni
1 tbs dill, finely chopped
Zest of ½ orange

Method

In a large casserole pot, heat the olive oil and sauté the onions for a couple of minutes. Add the calamari, wine, bay leaves, cloves, orange zest, cinnamon, grated tomatoes and 8 fl oz/240 ml of water. Season to taste. Simmer for 30 minutes or until the calamari is cooked.

In the meantime cook the risoni in water until tender. Drain the risoni and add to the cooked calamari and mix through.

Serve scattered with a little extra dill and orange zest.

Grilled octopus

Serves 4 to 6 people

Ingredients

1 (approx. 32 oz/1 kg) medium octopus, cleaned
Salt, to taste
Freshly ground black pepper, to taste
Olive oil
Dried oregano
Lemon wedges

Method

Place the cleaned octopus into a large pot of water, enough to cover completely. Simmer on a low heat for about 1 hour. Remove carefully, drain and pat dry.

Place on a hot grill or barbeque, turning over as it turns a golden color. You may prefer to cut the octopus into pieces before cooking or cut it after it has been cooked.

Arrange onto a platter and drizzle some olive oil over, sprinkle with dried oregano, season to taste with salt and freshly ground black pepper and lemon wedges.

Serve hot.

Shrimp and scallops with cherry tomatoes and peppers

Serves 4 to 6 people

Ingredients

10½ oz/300 g shrimp (prawns), peeled and deveined

10½ oz/300 g scallops, cleaned and halved

2 fl oz/60 ml olive oil

1 tsp sugar

1 red pepper (capsicum), diced

1 green pepper (capsicum), diced

17½ oz/500 g cherry tomatoes, halved

3½ fl oz/100 ml white wine

1 tbs dried oregano

2 cloves of garlic, finely diced

4 scallions (spring onion), thinly sliced

1 heaped tbs parsley, finely chopped

1 lemon, to serve

Salt, to taste

Freshly ground black pepper

Method

In a large frying pan heat the olive oil and sauté the scallions and garlic until soft. Add the pepper, tomato, oregano, sugar and wine. Mix well and simmer for 10–15 minutes. If it is getting too dry add 4 fl oz/120 ml of water. Add the shrimp and scallops, mix gently and continue cooking for another few minutes until the shrimp and scallops are cooked.

Season to taste. Serve with a drizzle of olive oil, a squeeze of lemon and a sprinkling of feta cheese and parsley.

Fried snapper

Serves 4 to 6 people

Ingredients

3½ fl oz/100 ml olive oil

*32 oz/1 kg whole snapper, cleaned (red mullet can
   also be prepared this way)*

5 oz/150 g plain flour

Salt, to taste

Freshly ground black pepper

Lemons for serving

Method

Wash and pat dry the snapper.

Place the plain flour on a plate and press the fish onto the flour until all sides are covered. Shake off any excess flour.

In a large frying pan heat the olive oil. Add the fish and cook on each side for about 6–7 minutes, or until golden and cooked through.

Season with salt and pepper and serve with lemon slices.

Salmon poached in olive oil

Serves 4 to 6 people

Ingredients

4–6 pieces of salmon
1¾ pint/1 L olive oil
Salt, to taste
Freshly ground black pepper, to taste
Fresh parsley, chopped roughly

Method

Place salmon in a large deep frying pan and pour over the olive oil until it covers the salmon. Poach on a low heat for approximately 20–30 minutes or until salmon is cooked. Carefully remove salmon from the oil and drain on some paper toweling.

Season with salt, freshly ground black pepper and sprinkle with parsley.

Serve with potato or green salad.

Grilled Sardines

Serves 4 to 6 people

Ingredients

12 sardines, cleaned
3½ fl oz/100 ml olive oil, for brushing and serving
2 tbs parsley, finely chopped
2 garlic cloves, finely diced
1 tbs capers
2 lemons, cut into wedges
Zest of one lemon
Salt, to taste
Freshly ground black pepper

Method

To make the marinade, in a large bowl use half the olive oil and add the parsley, garlic, lemon zest and capers.

Heat the grill and lightly brush with some olive oil. Place the sardines on the hot grill and brush with the marinade. Turn over after 2 or 3 minutes and brush again, cook for a further 2 to 3 minutes or until cooked.

Serve on a platter with lemon wedges and season to taste with the salt and pepper.

Snapper en papillote

'Tsipoura' is a fish that is widely used in Mediterranean cooking. Tsipoura as it is known in Greek is Sea Bream. You can also use fillets of king dory, blue eye, rockling, salmon and of course bream or whole baby snapper.

Ingredients

4 whole Snapper (14–17½ oz/400–500 g each)

3 oz/75 g pitted green olives, diced

2 fl oz/60 ml olive oil

1 small fennel, sliced finely keeping the fronds

4 tomatoes, sliced

2 tbs parsley, finely chopped

1 tbs dill, finely chopped

Salt, to taste

Freshly ground black pepper

4 pieces of greaseproof paper, large enough to hold the fish

Method

Preheat the oven at 400°F/200°C. Clean the fish well and dry with paper towels.

In a frying pan heat half the olive oil and sauté the sliced fennel for about 5–6 minutes or until soft. Season to taste.

Prepare the paper by cutting out squares large enough to hold the fish with enough room to fold over the edges to seal all the ingredients.

Fold paper in half, open up and place a quarter of the sautéed fennel in the centre on one side of the crease. Place one fish on the fennel and top with olives, sliced tomatoes, chopped parsley and dill.

Bring the other side of the paper over the fish. Beginning at one end of the opening fold over ½ in/1 cm of the edge. Keep folding all the way around the opening until it resembles a semicircle parcel. Repeat this to make the seal even tighter.

Place the parcels onto a baking tray and bake for about 20–25 minutes.

Serve on a large plate, slit open the parcel with a knife.

Perfect with a potato salad.

Calamari with macaroni

Ingredients

32 oz/1 kg calamari, cleaned and cut into small pieces
3½ fl oz/100 ml olive oil
1 onion, peeled and diced
1 clove garlic, finely diced
1 bay leaf
4 fl oz/120 ml red wine
14 oz/400 g tinned tomatoes

2 heaped tbs parsley, finely chopped
½ tsp paprika
½ tsp sugar
Salt, to taste
Freshly ground black pepper
9 oz/250 g short macaroni

Method

Sauté the onion in the olive oil in a large pot until soft. Add the prepared calamari, stir and cook for a few minutes or until the calamari changes color. Add the garlic, bay leaf, red wine, tomatoes and paprika, sugar and combine well. Bring to the boil, mix well then lower the heat and simmer for about 30 minutes. You can add some water if necessary, 8 fl oz/240 ml should be enough.

While the calamari is cooking, cook the macaroni in some water until tender and cooked through. Drain and add to the calamari when it is almost ready. Mix through well and serve with some extra parsley sprinkled over.

Lentil salad with salmon

Serves 4 to 6 people

Ingredients

7 oz/200 g green lentils

8 mushrooms, sliced thinly

1 carrot, grated

1 red onion, finely sliced

2 tomatoes, cut into chunks

6 slices smoked salmon or a piece of salmon poached in olive
  oil torn into chunks

3 fl oz/80 ml olive oil

1½ fl oz/40 ml red wine vinegar

Salt, to taste

Freshly ground black pepper

Fresh parsley and dill for serving

Method

Rinse the lentils under cold water and pour into a large saucepan with plenty of water to cover the lentils. Bring to the boil and simmer for about 15 minutes or until the lentils are cooked but still al dente, remove from the heat and allow to cool.

Place the cooked lentils in a serving bowl and add the mushrooms, carrot, onion, tomatoes and combine gently.

Pour the olive oil, vinegar and seasonings into a jar, close tightly and shake until blended. Drizzle over the salad and combine gently.

Top with the poached salmon (or smoked salmon) and an extra drizzle of olive oil and scattered with herbs for serving.

Meat and poultry

I love the meals that you can prepare earlier or even leave to slow cook. The succulent slow cooked meats and the one-pot casseroles are perfect for families, small and large.

Chicken fricassee

Serves 4 to 6 people

Ingredients

Chicken 1 – 1½ kilos cut into 8 pieces

2 fl oz/60 ml olive oil

4 scallions (spring onions), finely chopped

2 leeks, finely sliced whites only

2 iceberg lettuce, washed, dried and chopped into chunks

8 fl oz/240 ml white wine

2 tbs dill, finely chopped

1 tsp lemon zest

Salt, to taste

Freshly ground black pepper

Egg and lemon sauce (see recipe page 182)

Method

In a large deep frying pan heat the olive oil and add the chicken, browning on both sides. Remove the chicken and put aside. Using the same frying pan sauté the onions and leeks until soft. Return the chicken to the frying pan, add the wine, 8 fl oz/240 ml of water, lemon zest and the dill.

Simmer for about 20–30 minutes or until the chicken is almost cooked. Add the lettuce and simmer for a further 15 minutes. Season to taste.

Prepare the egg and lemon sauce and add it to the pan. Shake the pan a little to combine the sauce through.

Serve warm with fresh crusty bread.

Braised chicken with cinnamon

Serves 4 to 6 people

Ingredients

6 chicken thighs (on the bone and skin on)

3½ fl oz/100 ml olive oil

4 onions, quartered

2 large ripe tomatoes (peeled, seeded and diced)

1 cinnamon stick

20 black peppercorns

2½ oz/60 g currants

Salt, to taste

Method

In a large heavy saucepan heat the olive oil. Add the chicken and cook on a medium heat for 6–8 minutes or until lightly golden. Take the chicken out using a slotted spoon and place onto a platter. Add the onions to the saucepan and cook until softened, about 5–6 minutes. Return the chicken to the saucepan adding the tomatoes, cinnamon stick, peppercorns and currants. Add about 4–8 fl oz (120–240 ml) of water and season to taste.

Cover and simmer for 40 minutes or until the chicken is cooked. Serve with rice, pasta or potatoes. Serve hot.

Shoulder of lamb slow roasted

Serves 4 to 6 people

Ingredients

4½–5½ lb/2–2½ kg lamb shoulder
3½ fl oz/100 ml olive oil
2 tbs dried oregano
4 garlic cloves, crushed, skins left on
Salt, to taste

Freshly ground black pepper
8 fl oz/240 ml water
4 lemons (2 for juicing and 2 for serving)
4 potatoes, cut into large chunks (optional)

Method

Preheat the oven to 350°F/180°C. Place the shoulder of lamb in a baking dish, drizzle with the olive oil, squeeze over the juice of the 2 lemons, and sprinkle the oregano and season with salt and pepper.

Cover with foil and bake for approximately 1½ hours. Reduce the heat to 300°F/150°C and continue cooking for a further 2 hours. You can add the potatoes at this point if you are using them. Remove the foil, mix potatoes gently and cook in the oven for another 20–30 minutes at 350°F/180°C or until golden and cooked.

Season the potatoes and serve the lamb with extra lemon wedges.

One pot chicken with kritheraki (risoni) and spinach

Serves 4 to 6 people

Ingredients

4–6 chicken thighs
2 fl oz/60 ml olive oil
8 fl oz/240 ml tomato passata
1 small bunch of spinach, chopped
Salt to taste

Freshly ground black pepper
2 tbs parsley, finely chopped
17½ oz/500 g risoni

Method

In a large saucepan brown the chicken in the olive oil. Add the tomato passata and 16 fl oz/480 ml of water. Bring to the boil, and simmer for 10 minutes. Add the risoni and spinach and simmer for a further 15 minutes or until the chicken and risoni are cooked.

You can add a little more water if it is looking too dry.

Season well and sprinkle with the parsley. Serve with feta cheese.

Meatballs with cumin in tomato

Serves 4 to 6 people

Ingredients

3 fl oz/80 ml olive oil

17½ oz/500 g minced beef or veal

2 thick slices day old bread, crusts removed

4 fl oz/120 ml milk

1 onion, finely chopped

1 egg

2 heaped tbs parsley, finely chopped

½ tsp ground cumin

Salt, to taste

Freshly ground black pepper

Plain flour for coating

2 x 14 oz/400 g can diced tomatoes

½ tsp sugar

1 tsp oregano

1 tbs red wine vinegar

1 clove garlic, finely diced

Method

Place the bread in a bowl and cover with the milk. Leave until the milk has been soaked up.

In a large bowl place the mince, onion, egg, parsley, cumin and the bread (squeeze out any excess milk before adding). Season to taste and mix well with your hands or a wooden spoon. Take about a walnut size of mixture in your hands and mould into an oval shape.

In a frying pan heat half the oil and add the garlic and sauté for 1–2 minutes. Add the tomatoes, sugar, oregano and vinegar. Season to taste and simmer for 10–12 minutes.

In another frying pan pour the remaining oil and add the meatballs. Cook until golden, turning over so they are browned all over. Add the tomato sauce over and bring to the boil. Turn the heat down and simmer for a further 15–20 minutes. Shake the frying pan a little to make sure all the sauce is evenly distributed.

Serve with bulgar wheat, pilaf rice, pasta or potatoes.

Sweet things

Sweets are served on special occasions and for guests that may pop over for a coffee and stay a while.
Everyday dessert is always fresh fruit.

Homemade yogurt

Serves 4 to 6 people

Ingredients

4 pint/2 L full-fat milk
2½ fl oz/80 ml store bought natural yogurt

Method

In a large saucepan bring the milk to a boil. Turn the heat off and allow to cool until lukewarm. Take out 8 fl oz/240 ml of the milk and stir in the yogurt. This is used to make the culture. Pour it back into the pot slowly, mixing as you pour.

Pour the milk into cups, jars or individual bowls, whichever you prefer. Cover with some baking paper and cover with tea towels to keep warm for about 4 hours. I like to place a folded tablecloth on my kitchen bench, place my jars on it and cover with another tablecloth, so they keep warm all round.

The yogurt should be beginning to set. Place the jars into the refrigerator. The yogurt should keep for a week. You can keep some of your homemade yogurt to use as culture for your next batch.

I love my yogurt drizzled with honey and some walnuts.

Olive oil yogurt cake with honey yogurt

Serves 4 to 6 people

Ingredients

8 fl oz/240 ml olive oil
5 oz/150 g sugar
3 eggs
8 fl oz/240 ml milk
4 fl oz/120 ml Greek yogurt
3 oz/ 75 g golden raisins

Self-raising flour
Zest of half orange
16 fl oz/480 ml Greek yogurt
4 fl oz/120 ml honey
1 tsp vanilla extract

Method

Preheat oven to 400°F/200°C. Pour the oil into a large mixing bowl and add the sugar. Using an electric mixer whisk together. Add the eggs, one at a time. Pour in the milk and add the yogurt, continue mixing. Add as much flour as it needs to make a smooth cake mixture. Add the orange zest and the raisins. Mix well until combined.

Pour mixture into a prepared cake tin and bake for 45–60 minutes or until skewer comes out clean when inserted.

In a medium bowl place the yogurt, honey and vanilla extract. Mix well and set aside.
Serve at room temperature or cold with honey yogurt.

Diples

Ingredients

½ fl oz/20 ml olive oil plus oil for frying
3 eggs
9 oz/250 g plain flour
½ tsp baking powder
½ tsp vanilla paste
2 tsp cinnamon, for dusting
4 oz/110 g walnuts, finely chopped for sprinkling
1 tbs finely grated orange rind

Syrup

8 fl oz/240 ml honey
8 fl oz/240 ml water
1 tbs sugar
1 tbs lemon juice

Method

In a large bowl whisk the egg whites until fluffy, add the yolks and continue beating for another minute. Slowly begin adding in the flour and mix, add the baking powder and orange rind. Add the vanilla and olive oil, kneading well until dough is soft, elastic and not sticky. Place the dough in a floured bowl and cover with a tea towel, leave for 40 minutes in a warm room.

Sprinkle some flour onto your work surface and divide the dough into two. Roll out each ball of dough as thinly as you can. Cut strips approx 4½–5½ in x 3¼ x 10 in [12–14 cm x 8–10 cm]. Lay strips onto tea towels covered with extra tea towels to avoid drying up.

In a large frying pan pour oil at about ¾ in/2 cm deep on a medium-high heat. Using a fork pick up a strip of dough between the prongs and wrap it around the fork. Dip the fork into the boiling oil and swirl it around as the dough wraps around the fork. Remove the fork carefully and fry until golden brown. Remove with a slotted spoon draining any excess oil. Place onto a tray lined with absorbent paper. Repeat until all dough has been cooked checking the oil is not getting too hot.

Place the ingredients for the syrup into a saucepan, bring to the boil, skim off any froth and remove from the heat. Drop in the diples, one or two at a time and allow to stand for a minute, turning once, transfer to a serving dish. Have the cinnamon and walnuts in a bowl combined and sprinkle over the diples once they have been placed onto a serving platter.

Continue dipping into the honey and sprinkling with the cinnamon and walnut mixture until all finished. Delicious with a cup of Greek coffee.

Bougatsa with ricotta and sultanas

Serves 4 to 6 people

Ingredients

17½ oz/500 g ricotta cheese
5 oz/150 g sultanas
2 eggs
2 oz/50 g castor sugar
½ tsp ground cinnamon

Zest of 1 orange
3½ fl oz/100 ml olive oil
1 quantity filo pastry (you can make your
own or store bought)

Method

Preheat oven to 350°F/180°C. In a large bowl whisk the eggs and sugar until thick and creamy. Add the ricotta cheese and cinnamon and keep whisking. You can use an electric mixer if you prefer. When the mixture is light and fluffy, gently mix in the sultanas and orange zest and put aside.

Have your filo pastry on your work surface covered with a tea towel to prevent drying up. Place a sheet on your bench and brush with a little olive oil then place another sheet on top. Place two or three tablespoons of the ricotta mixture at the bottom ⅓ of the filo sheet, leaving a border on either side. Fold in the sides then fold the lower ⅓ up. Continue brushing with olive oil as you work. Finally fold the top ⅓ down, brush with the olive oil. You should have a rectangle parcel now.

Place onto a baking tray that has been brushed with olive oil and continue making parcels until all the mixture is finished. Sprinkle with a little water before you place in the oven.

Bake for about 15–20 minutes or until golden and crispy.

Serve at room temperature.

Rizogalo with yogurt and apricot conserve

Serves 4 to 6 people

Ingredients

5 oz/150 g medium grain rice
20 fl oz/600 ml full fat milk
1 oz/30 g cornflour
5 oz/140 g caster sugar

2 tsp vanilla extract
8 fl oz/240 ml Greek yogurt
Ground cinnamon, to serve
Apricot conserve (see recipe page 177)

Method

In a large saucepan boil 10 fl oz/300 ml of water. Add the rice and simmer over a low heat until the rice is cooked and the water is absorbed.

In a small bowl mix the cornflour with a little water to make a paste and add to the rice mixture, together with the sugar and vanilla extract. Add the milk slowly and keep stirring until it thickens. Take off the heat and stir in the yogurt, mixing well.

Pour into individual bowls or glasses and allow to cool. Top with the apricot conserve and sprinkle with cinnamon. Serve.

Fanouropita
(St Fanourio's cake)

St. Fanourio is the patron saint of lost things. Fanouropita is a cake made in honor of St. Fanourio on the Saints Day when it is made and taken to church for a blessing. This cake is also made many other times of the year, when searching for things that are lost such as jewelry or loves or when searching for an answer.

Ingredients

6 fl oz/180 ml olive oil

12 oz/350 g plain flour

1 tbs baking powder

1 tsp ground cinnamon

5 oz/150 g castor sugar

6 fl oz/180 ml orange juice

1 tsp vanilla extract

2½ oz/60 g raisins

2½ oz/60 g walnuts, chopped

Method

Preheat the oven at 350°F/180°C. Lightly oil a 9½ in/24 cm cake tin.

Place the flour, baking powder and cinnamon in a large mixing bowl and combine. Pour in the olive oil, orange juice and vanilla extract and using an electric mixer or a whisk mix well until all combined. Add the raisins and walnuts and mix gently.

Pour into the prepared cake tin and cook in the preheated oven for about 45 minutes or until the skewer that you insert comes out clean. Allow to cool a little before cutting.

You can dust it with a little icing sugar before serving if you like.

Apricot conserve

Serves 4 to 6 people

Ingredients

14 oz/400 g apricots, halved and pitted
2 tbs lemon juice
3 tbs sugar

Method

Combine apricots, lemon juice and sugar and put into a frying pan. Cook over a medium heat for 6–8 minutes or until syrupy. Transfer to a bowl until needed.

Herbal teas

Herbal teas are a nourishing refreshment, easily prepared and delicious. My favourite being the Greek Mountain Shepherds Tea as it reminds me of my mother who always had a pot brewing.

Ingredients

Mountain tea

Sage tea (faskomilo)

Linden (tilio)

Wild mint, Pennyroyal (fliskouni)

Camomile

Oregano

¾ oz/20 g dried herbal leaves and flowers

1¾ pint/1 l water

Method

Place the dried herbal leaves and flowers in a pot of boiling water and allow to infuse for a few minutes.

Strain and serve with a little honey, sugar, lemon juice, cinnamon or as is.

Sauces

Avgolemono or egg and lemon sauce, is the most famous sauce in Greek Mediterranean cooking – silky and tangy. It is used in soups, the most well known being the Chicken Avgolemeno soup. This sauce is also used to finish off many fish, meat and vegetables stews and some stuffed dishes such as stuffed zucchini.

Tselementes, one of the most influential chefs of his time and whose name is still synonymous to 'cookbook' introduced French style methods into Greek cooking and his most well known being the béchamel sauce.

Avgolemono (Egg and lemon sauce)

Ingredients

2 eggs
Juice of 1 lemon
A few tbs of juice from stock

Method

Lightly beat the eggs in a small bowl adding lemon juice gradually. Slowly add a little stock into the egg and lemon mixture beating all the time, add a little more stock, and continue mixing. Pour the egg and lemon sauce into your soup or dish stirring well so it doesn't curdle.

Béchamel sauce

Ingredients

4 tbs unsalted butter
1¾ pint/1 l full fat milk, warm
2 eggs
4 heaped tbs plain flour
Salt, to taste
Freshly ground white pepper
Pinch of grated nutmeg

Method

In a saucepan melt the butter and stir in the flour until combined. Pour the warm milk in slowly, stirring all the time as you pour, add the eggs and mix well. Add the nutmeg and season to taste.

Stir and cook until it is a custard consistency.

183

Z

Published in 2015 by
New Holland Publishers
London • Sydney • Auckland

The Chandlery Unit 009 50 Westminster Bridge Road London SE1 7QY United Kingdom
1/66 Gibbes Street Chatswood NSW 2067 Australia
5/39 Woodside Ave Northcote, Auckland 0627 New Zealand

www.newhollandpublishers.com

A catalogue record of this book is available at the British Library and the National Library of
Australia.

ISBN: 9781742576732

Managing Director: Fiona Schultz
Publisher: Diane Ward
Project Editor: Holly Willsher
Designer: Andrew Quinlan
Production Director: Olga Dementiev
Printer: Toppan Leefung Printing Ltd (China)

10 9 8 7 6 5 4 3 2 1

Follow New Holland Publishers on
Facebook: www.facebook.com/NewHollandPublishers

US: $19.99
UK: £14.99